15 RECITAL SONGS IN ENGLISH

Songs by
ARGENTO, BRITTEN, COPLAND, FINZI,
HEAD, IRELAND, QUILTER, ROREM
and VAUGHAN WILLIAMS

To access companion recorded accompaniments online, visit:
www.halleonard.com/mylibrary

Enter Code
4896-6718-2155-9452

BOOSEY&HAWKES

DISTRIBUTED BY

HAL•LEONARD®
7777 W. BLUEMOUND RD. P.O. BOX 13819 MILWAUKEE, WI 53213

www.boosey.com
www.halleonard.com

CONTENTS

Pianist on the recordings: Laura Ward

for Nicholas Di Virgilio

Dirge

from *Six Elizabethan Songs*

original key: a minor 3rd higher

WILLIAM SHAKESPEARE

DOMINICK ARGENTO

Largo e semplice (♪ = 60)

pp legatiss.

p dolciss.

Come a- way, Come a- way, Death, And in sad cy - press let me be laid;___

___ Fly a- way, Fly a- way, breath; I am slain by a fair cru-el maid.___

poco più mosso

My shroud of white stuck all with yew, O pre - pare it!___ O pre -

pare it!___ My part of death, no one so true Did___ share it.___

Did___ share it.___ Not a flower,

not a flower sweet On my black cof - fin let there be strown;___

To Beata Mayer

The Ash Grove

Welsh Tune

from *Folksong Arrangements Volume 1: British Isles*

original key: A♭ Major

Arranged by
BENJAMIN BRITTEN

sing-ing, I first met_ my_ dear one, the joy of my heart; A -

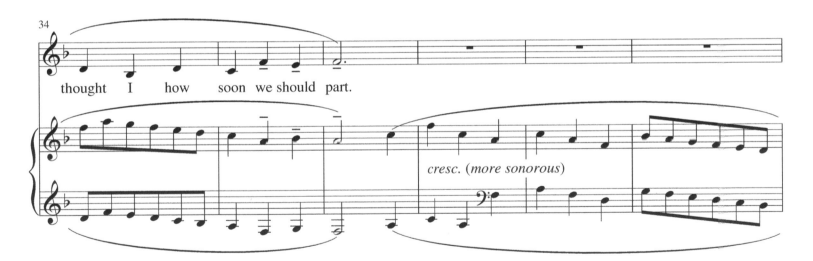

round us for glad-ness the blue-bells_ were_ ring-ing. Ah! then lit-tle_

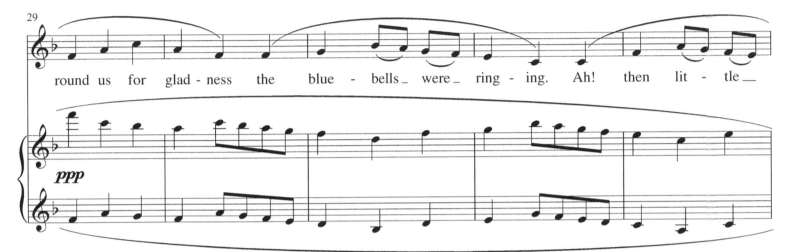

thought I how soon we should part.

cresc. (more sonorous)

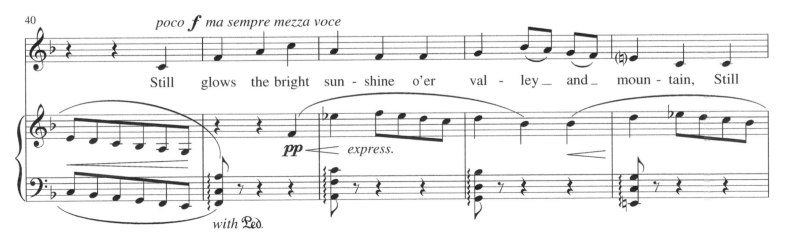

poco f ma sempre mezza voce

Still glows the bright sun-shine o'er val-ley_ and_ moun-tain, Still

pp express.

with Ped.

war - bles _ the _ black - bird his note from the tree; Still trem - bles the _

moon - beam on stream - let _ and _ foun - tain, But what are _ the _ beau - ties of

na - ture to me. With sor - row, _ deep _ sor - row, my bos - om _ is _

lad - en All day I_ go_ mourn - ing in search of my love. Ye

ech - oes, O tell me, where is the_ sweet_ maid - en? She sleeps 'neath_ the_

green turf down by the Ash - grove.

O Waly, Waly

from Somerset (Cecil Sharp) *

from *Folksong Arrangements Volume 3: British Isles*

original key: A Major

Arranged by
BENJAMIN BRITTEN

* By permission of Messrs. Novello & Co. Ltd.

row, my love and _ I. O, down in the
my my false love to _ me. A ship there

mead - ows the oth - er day, A - gath - 'ring flowers both fine and _
is, and she sails the sea, She's load - ed deep as deep can _

gay, A - gath - 'ring _ flowers both red and _ blue, I lit - tle
be, But not so _ deep as the love I'm _ in: I know not

thought what love can _ do.
if I sink or _ swim.

O, love is hand - some and love is fine, and love's a

jew - el while it is new, But when it is old, it grow - eth __

cold, and fades a - way like morn - ing __ dew.

To Clytie Mundy

The Salley Gardens

Irish Tune

from *Folksong Arrangements Volume 1: British Isles*

original key: G♭ Major

*W. B. YEATS

Arranged by
BENJAMIN BRITTEN

bid me _ take love eas - y, as the leaves grow _ on _ the _ tree, But _

I be-ing young and _ fool - ish with _ her did _ not a - gree.

In a field ____ by the _

riv - er my _ love and _ I did stand, And _ on my _ lean - ing _

shoul - der she __ laid her __ snow - white hand; She

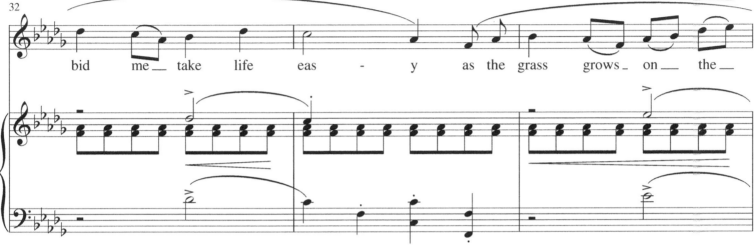

bid me __ take life eas - y as the grass grows __ on __ the __

weirs, But __ I was __ young and __ fool - ish, and __ now am __ full of

tears.

Simple Gifts

Shaker Song

from *Old American Songs, First Set*

original key: A♭ Major

Arranged by
AARON COPLAND

[2nd time to Coda]

love and de - light. _____ When true sim - pli - ci - ty is gained To

bow and to bend we shan't be a - shamed To turn, turn will be our de - light 'Till by

turn - ing, turn - ing we come round right. _____ 'Tis the

CODA

At the River

Hymn Tune

from *Old American Songs, Second Set*

original key: E♭ Major

Arranged by
AARON COPLAND

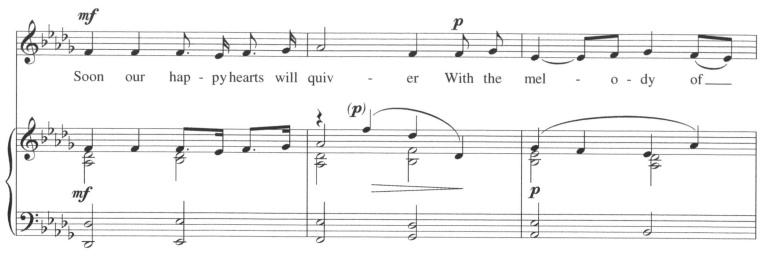

Soon our hap - py hearts will quiv - er With the mel - o - dy of ___

peace.

Yes we'll _ gath-er by the riv - er, The

beau - ti - ful, the beau - ti - ful ___ riv - er, Gath - er with the saints _ by the

riv - er That flows by the throne of _ God, ___ That flows by the throne of _ God.

Fear no more the heat o' the sun

from *Let Us Garlands Bring*

original key

WILLIAM SHAKESPEARE

GERALD FINZI

Fear no more the heat o' the sun,

Nor the fu - rious win - ter's rag - es; Thou thy

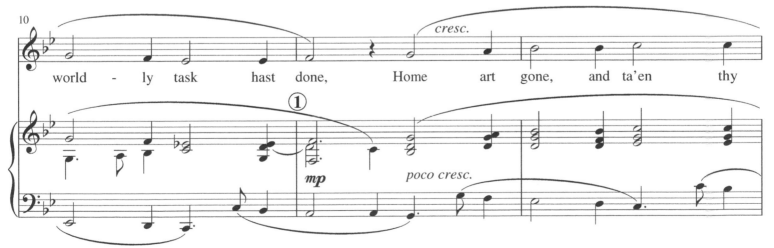

world - ly task hast done, Home art gone, and ta'en thy

No ex - or - cis - er harm thee! Nor no witch - craft charm thee! Ghost un - laid for - bear thee! Noth-ing ill come near thee! Qui - et con - sum - ma - tion have; And re - nown - èd be _____ thy grave! _____

Oh fair to see

from *Oh fair to see*

original key: a minor 3rd higher

CHRISTINA ROSSETTI

GERALD FINZI

Oh fair to see Fruit - la - den cher - ry tree, With balls of shin - ing red Deck - ing a leaf - y head; Oh fair to see!

a tempo

poco ritenuto al fine

1929
[1' 5]

To Hester Berry

Money, O!

from *Songs of the Countryside*

original key

W.H. DAVIES

MICHAEL HEAD

Then felt I like a child that holds A trum-pet that he must not blow Be- cause a man is dead; I dared Not speak to let this false world know. Much have I thought of life, and seen How poor men's hearts are ev - er light; And

Headley Down, Sept. 1928

Spring Sorrow

original key

RUPERT BROOKE

JOHN IRELAND

Poco andante

All sud - den - ly the wind comes soft, And Spring is here a - gain; And the haw - thorn quick - ens with buds of green, And my heart with buds of

*This Poem is reprinted from "1914 and other Poems" by Rupert Brooke,
by permission of the Literary Executor and Messrs Sidgwick and Jackson Ltd.*

pain. My __ heart all Win - ter lay so numb, The

poco cresc.

earth so dead and frore, That I nev - er thought __ the

Spring would come, Or my heart wake an - y more. But

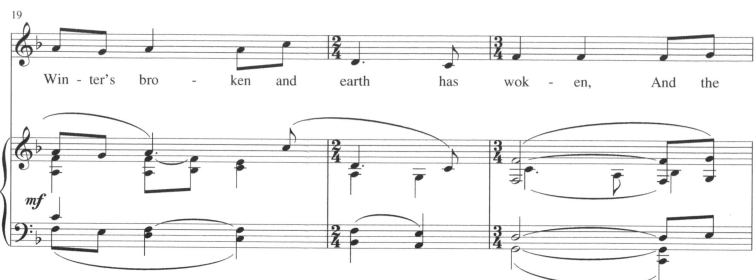

Winter's bro - ken and earth has wok - en, And the

small birds cry a - gain; And the haw-thorn hedge — puts forth its buds And my

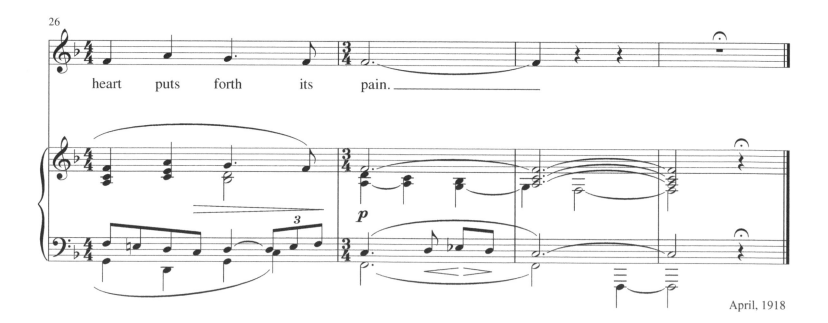

heart puts forth its pain. _____

April, 1918

To the memory of Arnold Guy Vivian

Drink to me only with thine eyes
from *Arnold Book of Old Songs*
original key: E♭ Major

BEN JONSON

English Melody
18th Century
Arranged by
ROGER QUILTER

To the memory of my friend, Mrs. Cary-Elwes

Weep you no more

from *Seven Elizabethan Lyrics*

original key: F minor

ANONYMOUS

ROGER QUILTER

weep - ing, That now lies sleep - ing, Soft - ly now

soft - ly lies Sleep - ing, sleep - ing.

Sleep is a re-con-ci - ling, A rest that peace be-

gets; Doth not the sun rise smil - ing When

fair at even he sets? _____ Rest you, then, rest, sad eyes! Melt not in

weep - ing, While she lies sleep - ing, Soft - ly now

soft - ly lies Sleep - ing, sleep - ing.

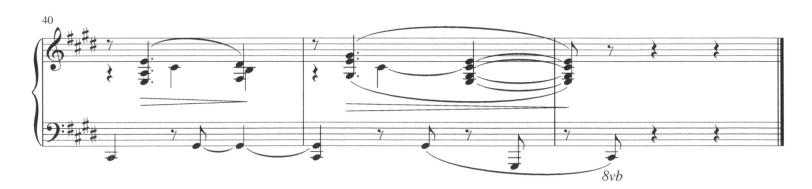

To Shirley Xenia Gabis Rhoads

Love
original key: E Major

THOMAS LODGE

NED ROREM

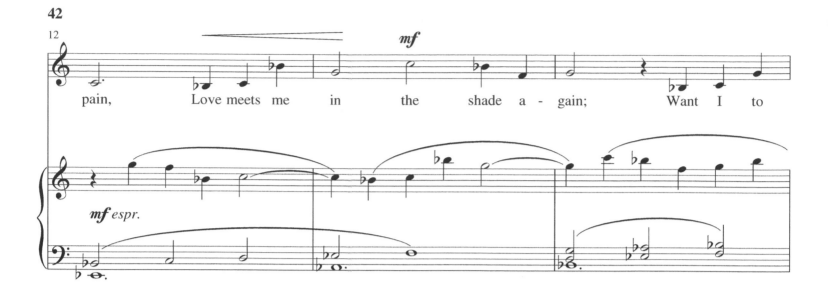

pain, Love meets me in the shade a - gain; Want I to

walk in se - cret grove, E'en there I meet with sa - cred

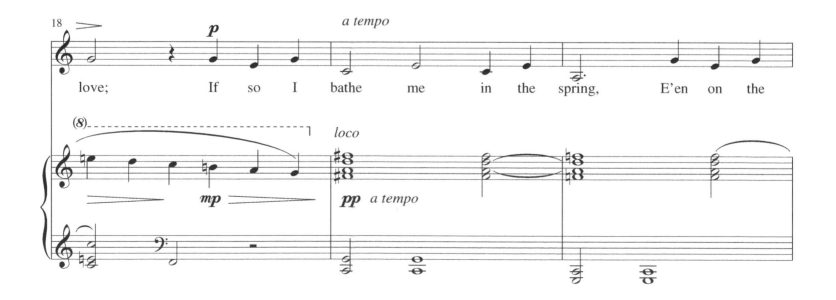

love; If so I bathe me in the spring, E'en on the

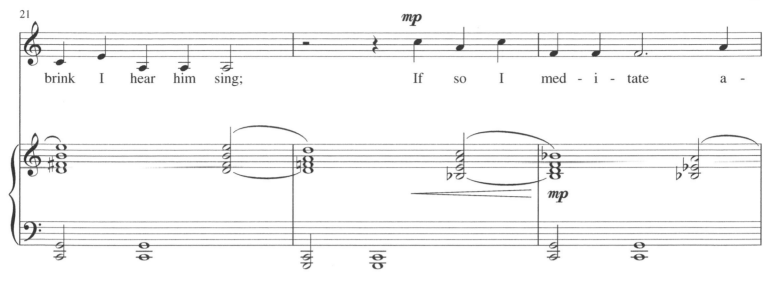

Hyères, 22 July 1953

To Nell Tangeman
Little Elegy
original key: E Major

ELINOR WYLIE

NED ROREM

With - out you No _ rose can grow; _ No _ leaf _ be _ green _ If _ nev - er seen _ Your _ sweet - est face; _____ No _ bird have grace _ Or _ power to sing; _ Or _ an - y - thing Be _ kind, _ or fair, _ And _ you no - where. _____

New York City, 28 March 1948
(Spring, cool, bright, noon)

Bright is the ring of words

from *Songs of Travel*

original key

ROBERT LOUIS STEVENSON

RALPH VAUGHAN WILLIAMS

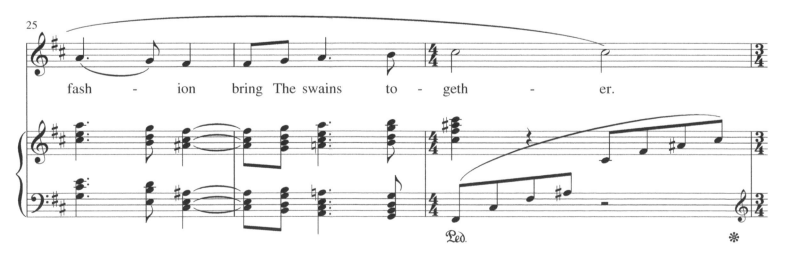